ATROPHY OF THE SOUL —
Mending a Broken Promise

Finding PATIENCE within the noise

"I wrote this not to rescue attention, but to restore Presence. To remind us to cultivate the fruit of the Spirit—PATIENCE, and allow it to serve as a modicum of awareness in these rather challenging times."

— Charles H. Jarvis, author of *"A Dozen Roses – The Relationship Challenge."*

Flow of Contents

Intro: A Timeless Wonder

First: Innocence of the Inner Sense

Second: Heaven's First Law

Third: A Lost Art

Fourth: Good Things

Fifth: Casualty of Impatience

Sixth: Seeing the Truth in Contradiction

Seventh: Spirits to Spiritual

Eighth: Nature's Embrace

Ninth: The Promise

Tenfold: A Meditative Heart

Foreword

In examining the work of Charles Jarvis, we encounter a masterful exploration of what befalls the soul when the foundational elements of relationship begin to erode. His earlier book, A Dozen Roses — The Relationship Challenge, offered a symbolic framework in which each rose represented a vital component of relational health: Respect, Listening, Anger, Trust, Sharing, Honesty, Patience, and others. Together, these twelve virtues formed a bouquet—an emblem of the delicate yet essential balance required for meaningful connection.

In his latest offering, Atrophy of the Soul — Mending a Broken Promise, Jarvis advances the conversation. He invites us to consider the consequences of neglecting these relational elements—not just in our partnerships, but in our inner lives. Just as a muscle weakens from disuse, so too does the soul falter when deprived of its moral and emotional nutrients.

Through a methodical and deeply insightful lens, Jarvis examines how modern society—rife with normalized transgressions and subtle betrayals—feeds the temptation toward spiritual decline. Yet this is not a lament; it is a call to awareness. With clarity and compassion, he identifies the causes of soul atrophy and offers antidotes that point toward healing: healthier relationships, restored integrity, and a more conscious society.

This book is not only a compelling read—it is a mirror, a map, and a meditation. It challenges us to confront the quiet erosion within and to seek renewal with intention and grace.

—Charles Stout

Introduction

A Timeless Wonder

"Self-Awareness"

Here we are at odds, where technology meets modernity, mass-curating perfection—masking imperfection; the soul—our quietest self—struggles to find its breath. What began as an innocent quest has become a cry. A longing for Patience in a world that no longer waits.

Amidst universal uncertainty, there was another, mine. As a world in spiritual decay pivots and turns, an inner reprimand, demanding quietude, calls for self-reflection.

It brought me back to the beginning of a journey that had already begun—authoring my first book, A Dozen Roses—The Relationship Challenge, which gave rise to something unexpected—an up-close and personal, in-depth look at self-doubt.

Line by line, page by page—what vulnerability exposed, brought forth chapters of emotions and memories that had lain dormant, whilst asleep.

In my many attempts to write, it wasn't just a creative challenge—it was a confrontation. An insecurity that dared me to ask: Who am I when everything else is stripped away?

Not just the surface me, but the honest, weathered spirit buried beneath the mind's chatter.

Unsure of how to start, the pages felt so intimidating and haunting at times—the rawness, the tears, the exposure.

Where was the blockage that dissuaded me?

Was it between pen and paper, heart and mind—was it my writing inabilities, or was it a hunger for validation playing a senseless game of Russian roulette with my fears?

This mission toward publication was years in the making, but it took shape in the desert sun of Phoenix, Arizona. I remembered staring mindlessly at the mountains, as I enjoyed doing—a backdrop radiating its own tranquility, hoping for a voice or a sign—something, anything—to turn my fears into wine.

There wasn't a playbook to follow, per se, in voicing the soul's cry. In hindsight, conquering my insecurity was a figuring out that had to be figured out.

In reflecting, it was as if a mystical energy catechized me, pushing me with a stick-to-itiveness that would invariably shove me over the hump—past the finish line. What held me up, entangled me, became clear. I—needed—to get out of my own way.

After a thorough chipping away of my conditioned responses, digging past the calcified build-up, I realized that contradiction was indeed my greatest adversary. After all, I wasn't just cooking for myself; this meal was meant to be shared.

So, in the kitchen I was, prepping, taste-testing, and slowly finding the confidence to trust my instinctual sensibilities.

Then came the moment of truth. It was as if faith had its own gestation period, giving birth to a renewal of sorts—a clarity of purpose and a spirit rejuvenated with a message.

'The Relationship Challenge' was finally inked, copyrighted, and etched into a Life-purpose.

It was like witnessing a curse flowering into a blessing, a deeply humbling experience.

Immersed in conviction, a conviction of a witness, looking back on how I free-dove into abandon, detached from everyday words, in search of hidden and deeper meanings, this meditation was a feast to context, adding tremendous expansiveness to perspective. It revived a curiosity that had washed up ashore, and above all, it reignited a flaming bonfire for learning.

'The Relationship Challenge' was timelessly evolving in real-time; its self-effacing ethos drew an even more mystical air.

I was comforted by a providential warmth, a protection bestowed upon a spiritual wanderer whilst exploring the foundational pillars of Respect, Trust, Honesty, and Patience.

The Relationship Challenge had opened up doors to rooms that had been closed, shut, cluttered, and unlit with dark memories from a fear of trying.

Some time had gone by, and I had gotten back into myself, so to speak, when one day, as I was perusing the chapter on Patience, I began to see more than I had written. One excerpt in particular kept returning.

"Hand in Hand is Love and Patience as Humility is to Grace. Flourishing is my Inner Sense; my Innocence is my Faith."

That phrase would not let go. "My Innocence is my Faith?"

It captivated me, so much that it made me ask: can Innocence be sustained in this digital age where disinformation blurs truth, where truth is a virtual portrayal?

Could it be preserved in a world susceptible to misinformation?

And could it be restored to its originality after it had been algorithmically compromised?

Moreover, I found myself entrenched in the inquisition.

So, I did what I've always done. I pressed forward, looking inward. As I delved in, beneath the surface layers, unsettlingly lurking in the background, was kind of a spiritual lethargy—a disconnection reminiscent of the collective soul, severely atrophied by the age-old struggle to be authentic, to think freely—to be who one truly is.

The algorithmic cloud cover polluting the airwaves had separated us into social groupings. The digital marketplace has now become a full-blown entertainment zone, offering 24-hour drive-thru service. All vying for a piece of the mind—or at least, what's left of it.

It pointed to the human condition with an insular blind spot, one yearning for relief from the superficial noise while eagerly seeking respite from the invasion of a pocket-sized perspective.

What was I sensing here? Where was Innocence taking me?

I felt disheartened, questioning whether Innocence was still possible or was living in the shadow of guilt, merely a sign of the times?

Did Possibility become an underdog, or was resentment driving a narrative contrary to a higher Love?

My query, My God!

Long gone is the stance from whence we sat. Time had changed. And candidly, I struggled with acceptance. Had the articulacy of the digital sphere intercepted the wits of one's natural disposition?

It certainly seemed that way. Things felt different. Unordinary. We were more connected than we'd ever been, technologically, yet cynicism was on the rise, and in togetherness, we were growing farther and farther apart.

What I sensed was not total despair by any means, but a command to look harder, go deeper, and listen keener. Know that, within every honest question, lies a seed of wisdom. It affirmed what I already knew. We are not doomed just yet. But pressed we are.

Pressed to snap out of apathy. Pressed to awake.

Pressed to protect the Innocent.

Pressed to uphold the Integrity of Inner Sense, especially on this virtual terrain. And atop these dreadful concerns, pressed to rediscover the awe and wonderment of curiosity.

As expressed in A Dozen Roses—The Relationship Challenge, the final gesture—"Your Success is my Success. Your Wellbeing is mine."—wasn't simply a closing statement. It was a conscious nod to a new beginning.

A vow extended beyond words; to restore the wellbeing of one is to shine a bright light on the collective spirit.

And that spirit?

The Atrophied Soul.

A disconnection in relationship. A desensitization of consciousness. A denaturing of the human touch. Not a visible breaking, but a subtle erosion—a spiritual thinning of our capacity to be present, to feel deeply, and to be patient.

Patience—like Innocence—is not weakness. It's a determination, an enduring thrust to thrive, a decrescendo of defiance in a world that demands expediency.

So—of all the roses, why begin with Patience?

May I share a story that pierces at the very heart of it?

I had traveled up to Scottsdale, Arizona, to visit a friend and mentor. Their lovely home was nestled in the desert hills, wide open to the majesty of the Sonoran landscape—Saguaro sentinels standing tall, Jumping and Teddy-bear

Cholla dotted along ridgelines under a sky of silent mystery, enough to hush any worry.

He was tending to his yard, with a reverence that simulated his humility, when he turned to me and said, "Hey, man, want to meet the little fella? My hummingbird?"

Before I could even open my mouth to respond, he started snapping his fingers and whistling—like he spoke a language only desert winds and wild wings understood. Then, unbeknownst to me, a hummingbird appeared from the vast desert. Not darting away in fear or circling around suspiciously, but gliding towards him, as if it were greeting a good friend.

It responded like they had known each other for years.

You could clearly see the bond. It wasn't unusual for this hummingbird to feed directly from the palm of his hands.

The magnitude of the moment—that pause between effort and trust—told me everything I needed to know about Patience.

W.O.W.

"Words of Wisdom" inspired by a moment.

Patience, like the hummingbird, doesn't arrive by force. It is welcomed by a stillness that signals safety. In our rush to achieve, prove, or preserve, we have forgotten this.

In this fast-paced, desire-it-now existence, Patience is often treated as a forgotten art. Yet, it is precisely this timeless virtue that holds the key to anchoring the deep roots of Humility, Grace, and Wisdom—Self-Awareness.

And notably, Patience does not wait idly. It awakens—slowly, silently, observantly—until readiness. Not shaped by opinion or validation, but by inner fidelity.

When one loses a Sense of Innocence, the soul bends under the weight of desolation. It droops like a rose left untended: once vibrant, now bowed by artificiality.

In a world that attempts to edit truth and manufacture connection, our fidelity to inner knowing begins to fade. We scroll, but rarely listen. We express light, but seldom see beauty.

Patience, like meditation, becomes not just a virtue—but a refuge. It teaches us how to return: to the Moment, to the Breath, into the Still. It does not raise its voice to be heard. It waits for us to lower ours.

That waiting? It becomes an offering that says, "Stay the course. Keep the Faith. Be a steward of the indivisible." This is not a plea for perfection, but for purpose. Not for rationale, but for reimagination.

Patience is more than a passage of time. It is the Soul of Understanding. The Heart of Perception.

    The Truth of Connection.

If Patience can earn the fulsome trust of an unsociable hummingbird living in the desert wilderness, could you imagine what this timeless wonder can do to reinvigorate a Soul atrophied by a Broken Promise?

First

Innocence of the Inner Sense

"Self-Inquiry"

Now that nearly every sector of life has been digitized—our information, our sacred texts, our education systems, and our entertainment; our emotions—the raw, natural sensibilities that once tethered us to truth prior to the erosion, our ability to think independently, falters.

In its place emerges a culture of imitation: despondent, distracted, and desperate. A flood of control substances enters the stream, attempting to restore the self-control we once possessed. But the damage runs deeper.

Materialism replaces meaning. Consumerism substitutes contemplation. Sensationalism displaces sincerity. We chase virality instead of vitality. We curate profiles instead of cultivating presence.

What was designed to mimic our likeness has, in turn, devalued our values, compromised our principles, and shortened the soul of relationship—the attention span.

Our shortcomings are sold as content. Our discontent becomes the currency of conjecture.

That which we once held close to the vest—wisdom, humility, patience—now stands on the brink of extinction in a marketplace thriving on manufactured thought and over-processed emotion. A culture of "hurry up and get on with it. Next."

Superficiality is no stranger to the human condition. Nor is pretense. The Relationship Challenge has always faced threats to a clear conscience, a good heart, and a healthy outlook. So surprised, we are not.

But the threats to our humanity have never been this invasive. This pervasive. This impulsive.

I was once asked, "What is the opposite of consciousness?" The person expected me to say "unconscious." To his surprise, knowing that consciousness has no opposite, I answered: "Compulsion."

And that compulsiveness is the heartbeat of the digital age.

It pulses through every scroll, every click, every notification. It reeks of bad intentions masked as innovation. It seduces the soul with speed, spectacle, and simulated connection.

We are not merely just losing our minds. We are forfeiting our essence. Yet amid the buzz—of social media, artificial intelligence, and the endless stream of innovation—there lies a quieter truth.

These tools offer tremendous benefits and reward. Research. Cost reduction. Efficiency. Connectivity. We've all caught the buzz. But not all things are duplicable. Not wisdom. Not presence. Not the soul's silent unfolding.

And that is why, now more than ever, one must cultivate the virtue of Patience—and exude the courage to be still.

Stillness is like the wind. Invisible, yes. But indispensable. It does not clamor for attention. It does not trend. It does not notify. Yet without it, we unravel.

To deepen understanding and broaden awareness, one must reclaim the capacity to be still. To find balance. To create harmony, space to evolve, not just accelerate.

Stillness is not inaction. It is the pause between impulse and insight, a choiceless one. It is the breath before creation. It is the soil in which virtue takes root.

In a world addicted to immediacy, stillness becomes an act of resistance. A spiritual practice. A relational necessity.

The Relationship Challenge faces its most formidable obstacle yet: Being yourself in a digital age.

When identity is curated, not nurtured—where our profiles become extensions of our ego, and interconnectedness is digitized, Understanding itself becomes a fragile thing—half-empty or half-full, depending on who you ask, or which algorithm decides what you see.

This brings us to a haunting question: Can the innocence of the inner sense survive?

Can it endure the algorithmic cloud that hovers over our every thought, every impulse, every longing?

The inner sense—once intuitive, relational, unanimously recognized as pure and good—now competes with metrics. It is interrupted by notifications. It is shaped by trends.

We are taught to optimize, not empathize. To perform, impersonally. To scroll, and stroll, not sit still. And the soul, once the inner haven of wisdom, becomes noisy with hollow impressions and projections.

But the inner sense is not easily extinguished. It is patient. It is persistent. It perseveres. It waits beneath the noise, like a firefly in the dark—small, luminous, and unbothered by the algorithm. In fact, its algorithm is faith.

Innocence.

What is Self-knowledge without Self-understanding?

This is an inquiry one must undertake; to do so is to accept The Relationship Challenge.

Here, one must be open and willing to examine the nature of the unknown.

To speak of brokenness is not to condemn—it is to confess. To acknowledge that something integral has been interrupted. That the thread between soul and self has frayed. And yet, even in fragmentation, the inner voice still whispers with a wholesome tone.

The Relationship Challenge invites us to listen for that whisper. To trace the symptoms of dis-ease back to their spiritual root. Not merely to treat, but to understand. Not merely to cope, but to connect. Because health is not just the absence of illness, it is devotion.

It is the soul's ability to remain whole in a world that profits from our pieces.

So when asked, "How is your health?" We are not asking for numbers or metrics. We are asking: Are you at peace with yourself? Are you in harmony with others? Are you devoted to something greater than self-absorption?

The Relationship Challenge is not a test. It is an inquiry—a constant state of learning. The sensibility of innocence. A restoration of the original algorithm—Intuition.

As we look within ourselves, answering the question of Faith—of Love—of Health, while the inner voice tells us everything we need to know, it doesn't hurt to consult definition.

What is health? It's the challenge we all face. From cut to fade. The conscious to the unaware. Till death do us anew. This is why we say Relationship is everything.

Health is everything!

Some say health is wealth. Others say wellness is living your best life. And I say, "Your wellbeing is mine." But I like to go straight to the heart of the matter—to a definition that spans centuries—covering its vast field—our happiness.

Whole. Harmony. Balanced

Sane. Clarity. Connected.

Holy. One. Devoted.

Integral. Holistic.

Spiritual.

When asked, "How is your health?" You're inadvertently asking, "How is your Relationship?"

In the original book, "A Dozen Roses — The Relationship Challenge," 'Your wellbeing is mine' also means in sickness. To address health, it must be done patiently, with empathy, and with compassion.

It's an awareness of dis-ease.

Distress. Inflammation. Imbalance.

Fear. Anxiety. Stagnation.

Unfaithful. Unhopeful. Discontentment.

Flawed. Fragmented.

Broken.

What is the Broken Promise?

The Broken Promise is not honoring the difference between time and the timeless.

Health is timeless. It's not treating the Mind, Body, and Spirit as separate entities—instead as one.

One flow. One energy. One existence.

Health, then, is not a trend. It is a Spiritual Practice. It's more than physicality; it's a daily devotion to Wholesome Living. It's not just mentality; it's Observation.

It's the honorability of Stillness. The Innocence of the Inner Sense.

And Patience—Patience is the virtue that makes this practice flourish. It is a resilience that perseveres through fragmentation. It is the spiritual posture that allows healing to unfold—not on our schedule, but on the soul's time.

To be Patient is to trust the Timeless. To be Healthy is to live in Oneness. And to mend the Broken Promise is to Look Within Yourself and remember, 'Relationship is Everything!'

The best indicator of who we are is seen through it. Regardless of what we think of ourselves, relationships have the final say.

What does it mean to be true to yourself?

It's a Knowing.

A continual deepening of Self-understanding. A lifelong broadening of Self-awareness.

As innocence flickers beneath the algorithmic haze, we turn toward Order—not as control, but as remembrance.

If innocence is the seed, how must we till the inner sense to let it flower?

Second

Heaven's First Law

"Self-Knowing"

Her Spirit lives.

It's kept alive by a knowing.

A connection.

A deep, abstract understanding, similar to that of faith.

Not retention, but the vision peeking through humility. A lust for the unknown, which instilled confidence into a mind struggling to conform.

With a posthumous message stating, "Have order." Oh, and "don't forget to be gracious."

I recognize how privileged I was to have grown up with mantras such as "Order is Heaven's first law" and "To know Love, you must first know what it's not."

These words were not just spoken; they were exercised and role-modeled, and drilled into a budding consciousness.

Like a spiritual griot, my grandmother was a disciplinarian by trait to the truest sense of the word.

Discipline meaning 'a student of faith.'

A natural teacher.

Self-taught.

Strict.

Stern.

Steady.

A beacon of wisdom outpouring from her eternal soul.

She could interpret scripture in a way that saved us from ourselves. A memory of a hummingbird. You know, the ones that would leave for months and return just in time for a seasonal bloom.

Yes, a sharp instinct.

Intuitive.

Very intellectually gifted!

Her name was Evelyn, but we called her Sista. She was very private and did not covet much attention.

She was a devotee.

We shared an unbelievably strong bond.

I never asked why we called her Sista, but as a practicing Christian, I'm willing to guess that in keeping with the tradition of 'we're all brothers and sisters,' she was seen as a vessel of that light.

Sista was a staunch proponent of thinking for yourself. Growing up in the Caribbean—Nevis to be exact, it wasn't uncommon to be showered with anecdotes, euphemisms, storytelling, and scripture, keeping us in line.

Nurturing common sense was high on the list of what was required to be a good person.

Order, Heaven's first law, was both rod and staff, shepherding that goodness.

I reflect with supreme adoration of her raw excellence.

Being brought up in a Christian household wasn't a bubble by any means. Our little island was a microcosm of the larger society.

There was a strong religious influence of Roman Catholicism. With its British colonial history, the Anglican Church was the local house of worship for us. There were also the Methodists, the Seventh-day Adventists, Pentecostal, Jewish influences, and space for non-believers, along with other African-rooted Spiritual Traditions.

The little island sat like a religiously philosophical melting pot.

Graced with Sista's presence, Self-respect wasn't just taught—it was witnessed. It stood like a flame at the center of every relationship, casting light into corners where indifference once lurked. That light demanded discernment. It asked: Are you centered? Or are you simply self-involved? The answer lay not in pride, but in awareness.

To walk through life with Order meant choosing presence over dominance, patience over panic, discernment over destruction. We didn't always speak these truths aloud—but we lived them, in humility, and when necessary, defiantly.

"To know Love, you must first know what it's not." This wasn't merely wisdom—it was survival. The Relationship Challenge wasn't a test of charm or compatibility; it was a spiritual evocation requiring filters of innocence. Control, criticism, comparison—these were telltale signs of Disorder, the fingerprints of a fractured soul trying to masquerade as the chosen one.

In our village, intelligence wasn't measured by knowledge alone, but by how deeply you understood what to walk away from. A careless word. An unjust gesture. A transactional kindness. If you walked away with grace intact, the elders knew. The word traveled. You were seen as one who carried Order.

Negation, as it turns out, was as holy as an act. Not bitterness, not arrogance, but a "no thanks" to all that disfigured Love. The empath didn't earn their name through emotion alone, but through the disciplined art of saying: "This is not mine to carry."

Negating the false was to negate fear.

You learned quickly that Balance wasn't a midpoint between good and bad. It wasn't compromise—it was self-worthiness. To confuse the two would risk spiritual drift. The wise knew that—where Hate did not dwell, where Comparison had no echo, where Control could not trespass, Love is.

Care was the centerpiece. Not as sentiment, but as vibration. An unmetrical geometry of concern, receptivity, and watchfulness.

That was Sista's gift—she didn't just observe, she attended. She didn't discipline for appearance; she disciplined to restore order. She was steady as sunrise, sharp as scripture, and quiet like the hummingbird that returns when the soul has bloomed enough to receive it.

To be a Caregiver of Goodness under her guise was to become a steward of frequency. You learned to read conduct like music, with Order as the melody and Relationship as its rhythm. That's what we danced to. That's what we called harmony.

And so Order—Heaven's First Law—wasn't something you performed. It was something you cultivated, something you embodied.

In Sista's words, "Cleanliness is next to Godliness." But cleanliness, for her, wasn't preparation for the afterlife; it meant purity of intent. No cluttered motives. No chaotic desires. Just a clear path to goodness.

Order negated Disorder. Love rejected illusion. Self-respect cuts through indifference.

At the heart of it all—the Spiritual Practice of Discernment, where knowing what Love is not leads you to what Love truly is.

Self-knowing.

And what is 'Care' without Self-knowing?

Self-knowing isn't just inner awareness—a gut instinct; it's intellectual independence. It's the ability to stand before consensus, customs, or comfort, and say, "Let me see for myself." Sista modeled this so intuitively, not by rebellion, but through wisdom—a propensity for truth, with discernment, and a disciplined art of questioning.

To think for yourself is to guard the soul against automation—be it cultural, relational, or ideological. It's how intuition finds structure. And when paired with the observation of what love is not, it becomes a spiritual filtration system: sensing what's off, refusing what's hollow, and choosing what's whole.

Self-knowing, then, becomes a dance between soul-trust and soul-proof. You listen deeply to your inner voice—and you ask boldly, "Does this resonate with love?" "Or does it carry the weight of disorder?"

Thinking for yourself is not isolation—it's autonomy. And when done rightly, it is the highest form of Care.

Heavenly.

Orderly.

One cannot be themself in the past. One cannot see for themselves through filters. One cannot yield to understanding without Self-knowing.

With Order as our breath and conscience as our map, we begin to walk—not toward perfection, but with presence.

Third

A Lost Art

"Self-Respect"

The title "Atrophy of the Soul" did not arrive out of thin air—it arose out of a collective exhaustion.

Not from ambition, nor from aesthetic aim, but from a long, aching meditation on what we had become. We, the overstimulated. The overconsuming. The spiritually overdrawn. Overreacting, really—in an overprocessed manner on a virtual terrain.

There was once a silent moment in our homes. Not silence from absence, but peace from presence. Now, every room flickers with the spectral glow of the digital. Even our sanctuaries—those sacred, velvet-lined spaces of governance and prayer—have become assembly lines for urgency and spectacle.

And I? I stood dismayed. Disheartened. Not yet defeated, but heavy in my chest, and did what was called upon to do. I picked up my armor—

my pen—and wondered how to chart a chant for restoration.

What do you call restraint when it's no longer in fashion? What do you call purpose when it doesn't trend? What do you call defiance when it is quiet, enduring, and rooted in patience?

The depletion of the inner consciousness is not a new phenomenon. On the island, we sang Glen Campbell's 'Try a Little Kindness' with spiritual fervor. The Jamaicans gave it a reggae vibe, a dancing rhythm. The rhythm gave it urgency. And the words— "You've got to try a little kindness..."— They met our ears like scripture, braided from the Deep South to the Ocean Blue Souls of the Caribbean.

"You've got to try a little kindness, Yes, show a little kindness. Just shine your light for everyone to see. And if you try a little kindness, then you'll overlook the blindness. Of narrow-minded people on the narrow-minded streets."

But now, even those streets—those narrow-minded streets—have been digitized. And kindness, I fear, has been compressed to pixels, its warmth reduced to reactions.

We speak of atrophy, and some may imagine limbs. But I have seen the soul wither. Through social distancing, social discourse, social warfare—and through the war we wage silently against ourselves with every swipe, every scroll, every forgotten breath.

Do not mistake my lament as blame. I do not exile myself to the hills and valleys—though I do hear the quiet there more clearly. This is not a sermon from solitude. It is a reflection from within the noise.

The disconnection must be challenged. The desensitization can't be ignored. And the denaturing of our lifestyles, the dis-ease is real.

We sleepwalk through daylight. We sleep-talk through relationships. We daydream through devotion.

We are sleeping whilst awake. And the art we've lost may be the art that once saw who you really are.

Not so long ago, the fiercest threat to the home was the soft glow of television screens—entertainment turned uninvited tenant. One in every room, like surveillance. And though its signal was analog, its impact was personal. It split the house into tribes. Preferences over presence. Characters over kin. We watched, we reclined, we fell into a comfort—not in awe, but in a snooze.

Back then, concerned citizens circled the wagons around a now-familiar refrain: What is happening to society?

We managed to keep pace, or so we thought. But now, we are not just viewers—we are the content. Overconsumed, overwhelmed. Our attention fractured, our tempers threadbare, our souls abbreviated.

Discontent has become our muse. Endless content creation from inner chaos. And what used to be discretionary is now public consumption.

Chivalry?

Long thought dead—today, it's buried under hashtags and hollow hearts. The marketplace is open 24/7, but our hearts are closing in need of resuscitation.

Where did the courtesies go—the gentle ones, the unassuming ones? The ones that didn't need likes to be liked?

Some say that a global catastrophe is our greatest threat. But isn't it the relational climate? When we no longer see each other, really see—no longer value the wonder of another soul?

What we call privacy loss may actually be the empathy famine. Our lives made public, but our hearts remain unpublished.

"They say the kids nowadays don't have any manners." "I say their parents misplaced the patience to teach it—busy curating relevance."

As we sink further into this digital abyss—this dark matter of the mind—we surrender something sacred.

Responsibility. Believability. The grit of Integrity.

And once those slip through the cracks, confidence becomes a steep hill to climb. Some things are non-negotiable. I believe humility is one of them.

In my compound—tongue firmly in cheek—it wasn't just custom, it was covenant. "Good night" was an evening sacrament. No muttered phrases. No distracted nods. Eyes met. Spirits acknowledged. Grace given and returned.

This was no bedtime cliché—it was a ritual for home training, as it was called. Not dictated by age, but by intention. A good night filled the room like incense. And in the morning, nature returned the favor.

Good morning! The rooster crowed blessings. Good morning, rooster.

Grunting pigs made their peace. Good morning, piggies.

The hens laid abundance. Good morning, chickies.

The breeze danced through the trees. Good morning was gentle as the wind.

Good morning! The sheep, guardians of innocence, birthed little ones. And when the lambs arrived, so did awe. A hush fell over the earth, signifying—Good morning, a new life had begun.

A Good Morning was apropos to a Good Day, to having Good Manners—the essence of excellence. A blueprint for belonging. A cadence to Self-respect.

Let me tell you about a conversation I had with my brother, DJ, who is one of the kindest and most lovable people I know. The testimonials are evidentiary if you've been lucky enough to meet him.

So I thought, who better to pose the question of good manners to?

I remembered asking him, "Yo Deej, why is having manners important?"

His poignant response was spat out instantly. "Dude, manners have taken me to Australia and back." Full stop. For context, my brother does not live in New Zealand, if you get my drift.

Good manners boost understanding. They calm doubt and prevent negativity. DJ led Good Manners into a deeper level—not just etiquette as tradition, but manners as kindness.

A gesture, a tone, a friendly acknowledgment of others. His words were brilliant in their simplicity: "Manners have taken me to Australia and back." That is supporting evidence that kindness has no limitation.

Can manners reconnect us to our roots and bring us back to a time when 'eye-to-eye' contact meant more than just acknowledgment?

Good Manners: a tapestry woven with discernment, discretion, and interconnectedness.

The Soul's Signature. Yes—and beautifully so. Springing from awareness, in honor of another's humanity.

Discernment sees. Discretion shields. Mind your Manners, please. A combustion of emotional intelligence that can't be faked, only realized.

A beginning that invites dignity. An ending that leaves the door open. Good Manners aren't decoration—they're relational architecture. Likeability rooted in grace, not charisma, not charm.

It's the small acts. The big impression. The pause, the gesture, the "please," the "thank you." These are relational cues that say, "You matter. I am aware."

Good manners reduce suspicion. Break down barriers. And discourage toxicity.

They welcome hospitality.

Good manners are not tactics. They are temperature. They signal emotional weather, offering shade to the burdened and warmth to the estranged.

They speak before you do. They linger after you've gone. They are the quiet poetry of likeability. What makes someone lovable is not just how they speak, but how they listen, gesture, wait, and respond.

Discernment reveals what's true. Discretion protects what's tender. But manners?

Manners deliver Truth with Dignity.

Ask DJ.

There are souls whose grace enters before their words do. Their manners are not scripted—they are guided by innocence. They listen with their whole body. They leave footprints, not fingerprints. DJ embodies this ritual well, not out of obligation, but through intuitive warmth.

Manners, when worn with truth, become the most traveled passport of all.

Good manners do not ask who you are. They remind you that you are. A presence that says, "come on in."

From the child scribbling in the margins of Sunday school to the scholar housed in the Library of Congress, and from the grocer who greets without pretense to the premier who bows in humility, all are met with the same tone of respectability—genuine, grounded, and gracious.

Let this be the year manners spread far and wide. That "Good morning" has more healing power than it commands. May genuine and simple recognition restore what performance cannot.

May the universal salutation of "Good morning" serve as a cultural offering.

In every language and tone, carrying on tradition with the warmth of words passed down, spoken humbly to honor lineage, and conveying to others: My fellow Human, I see you in the light of day, and I respect your place in it.

A subtle way of saying, I care that you're here. Glad that you are awake. Happy that you're alive.

Let it be Food for the Soul—offered not because it's owed, but because it's earned through Self-respect, moving from a Lost Art to a reformed blessing.

The morning doesn't require spectacles. It demands sincerity. And a "Good morning" spoken with grace becomes a sign of mutual respect, turning greetings into gateways.

And "Thank You" into Kindness.

"Good morning!"

As we lie bare in the ruins of overstimulation, we begin again—not with noise, but with a vow of silence.

A vow to love thy neighbor.

Fourth

Good Things

"Self-Worthiness"

Nature cannot be rushed.

Rain falls when it must. Seeds are ready when they burst. The sun warms the soil not by choice, but by assignment. This rhythm is not just seasonal—it's spiritual.

Shall we dance to it?

To bear witness is to recognize the invisible dance between time and transformation.

Patience in nature isn't stagnation.

It's gestation.

It's the slow, deliberate swell beneath the surface, the invisible stirrings of life preparing to reveal itself. And so, too, within us, there is a soil beneath the skin, an inner knowing that breaches turmoil in response to understanding.

That fruitfulness living deep within our heartland blooms through acts of care, retreats in moments of haste, and flourishes when nurtured with an unconditional hand. When we attune ourselves to this cycle, waiting becomes a meditation.

Not time-binding—time-sensitive.

Watchful.

The leaf doesn't rush to unfurl. The river does not hurry to meet the sea. And perhaps our own growth, our becoming, our evolving—deserves the same succinctness.

Shall we walk barefoot through the garden of discovery?

As trailblazers, tiptoeing through the rocky terrain of uncertainty, we must acknowledge that 'good things come to those who wait.'

Those who are patient enough to walk alone— walk the providential trails of virtue.

Abiding.

Observing.

With privilege.

Nature's way of sanitizing and sensitizing the soul.

Growing up in the heart of a tropical haven, steeped in spiritual abundance—not the kind wrapped in luxury, but the kind that was earthed—uncurated, uncommercial, unhurried.

From free-falling coconuts that thudded like time itself landing in the dirt, to guavas aromatically ripened with a nocturnal witness, to mouth-watering tamarinds whose tartness stung with nostalgia. It was Eden without ceremony. Hedonism without sensationalism.

This wasn't just a garden—it was a classroom. And nature, our elder teacher, never lectured. She simply presented the lesson: that Patience fertilizes Purpose. That fruit isn't rushed to ripen, and water without conservation is land at waste.

We learned to taste the weather. To feel the texture of the season not through a screen or forecast, but in our mouths, under our feet, in our breath. We understood that what humans endeavored came to fruition when the elements cooperated. And when they don't, the roots of humanity grow stronger—with faith.

What's cultivated in this garden was a schooling in observation, in taking risks, and the humility of privately giving thanks. Not everyone had a front-row seat to such an orchestra—where the sun conducts, the rain harmonizes, and the soil sings with promise. But even when the garden song fades, its melody still hums. The clouds still danced.

Before we understood prayer by virtue, we knew its name. Not from scripture, but in the raising of sugar cane. The ripening of mangoes. The flood or flourish of cassava.

Nature did not seek belief. She demanded observation—and then rewarded our involvement with wisdom. We recognized this bounty not as guarantee, but as an edict of glory.

The land was a co-op, a covenant, a relationship. Our hands worked the soil, but it was the heavens that watered it. And when the fruits multiplied tenfold, when the rains came not to ruin but to replenish, the voices rose in exultation: "Thank you, Jesus." Not just a phrase, but a chant of joy praising every harvest, every meal, every mouthful.

Even scarcity had meaning. Drought taught the dryness of austerity—admonishing us to do our part and trust what was yet possible. And that trust—that unseen partnership—was the first prayer of participation.

The garden was indeed a playground, a classroom, and a sanctuary all in one.

Nature's showcase symbolized that spring had arrived and thy kingdom come. I still reminisce in good faith and with the most profound sentiment of gratitude.

Wouldn't you, if you saw wild fruits hung like ornaments from trees, welcoming the season?

Coconuts falling unannounced, cracking open the sweet refreshment of a warm day's reprieve. Red and yellow cashews perfumed the air with dazzling confidence, while pomegranates split open like secrets, revealing their jeweled truths.

Then, there was the source of vitality, the soursop, that soothed the belly with its cream-like consolation—a fruit with a flavor of milky joy. Passion fruits? They were the hummingbird of the fruit species, bursting with conviction, proving that even the smallest vessel could house the soul of summer memories.

Mangoes, ripe and radiant, descended into our hands like gifts—no exchange, no payment, just presents. The talk of the town.

The guineps bunched with mouthwatering delight were the steal of the summer, and tamarinds hung like earrings, teaching us to value sour before sweet; it rewarded maturity.

Finger bananas curved like smiles, playful and approachable. Plantains offered sustenance, linking soul to tradition and tradition to food. And the avocados—hmnnn, they were monuments of tenderness—reminded us that slow growth is long and abundant.

Papayas—the buffet of the wilderness was a shared enjoyment.

Below the trees, ground provisions took root with quietude. Potatoes and yams burrowed into the soil, unseen but unshaken. Cassava taught us that strength comes in layers. Wild pumpkins, with their rugged beauty, lent the garden its earthy pride.

Then there was the 'Shack Shack' tree—the Royal Poinciana, or more scientifically but still regal, the Delonix Regia, with all of its seasonal flamboyance. Its floral sensation and long pods that dangled like wind chimes, singing in the breeze, instilled musicality. Its presence attracted hummingbirds, bumblebees, and lizards whose colors camouflaged them as we looked up in amazement.

When the pods dried out, they became musical, similar to the spiritual accompaniment of the tambourine. As kids, we found the gospel within and sang 'Ha—lle—lu—jah, Ha—lle—lu—jah, Ha—lle—lu—jah, Ha—lle—lu—jah.'

This was nature's inheritance. A tropical bounty that asked only one thing in return—observance. The festival of fruits gave us a taste of the season, as the colorful hibiscus decor with jubilation. When we closed our eyes, the texture of the tropical weather massaged our skin with rejuvenation.

There was an understanding that what is cultivated must first be permitted by Mother Earth.

We did not harvest with haste. We harvested with a taste for gratitude.

"Good things come to those who wait" was not a wait-and-see approach, but rather a call to participate.

Involvement.

It was a season of preparation, the slow unfurling from uncertainty to sustenance.

To wait was not with deviled hands, impatience—even though filled with anticipation.

You worked incessantly in alignment with Nature's plan. To learn that readiness isn't something you wait for; it's something innately agreed upon in relationship with time and truth, with nature, with everyone.

Patience, then, is not just endurance.

It's dedication.

The good things in life don't arrive by wish or whim. They come through resilience—through the devoted tending of Soil, Soul, and Spirit.

Nature never makes promises. Her presence offers us restorative and regenerative gifts. She teaches us to nurture with open hands and a guarded heart, knowing that abundance can quickly turn to mud with a shift of a cloud, darkening over the sun.

And yet, we remained devoted. Not because we were promised manifestation, but because you were the connection, commitment, from source to affection.

To treat relationships—human or elemental—with the same awe we reserved for a mango tree in bloom, or a rainfall after drought, was the sprouting of the seed of wisdom.

Nature wasn't just a guide. She was a mentor in faith. Her bounty gave us firsthand accounts of hope, but her storms reminded us of humility. And through both, we learned that nothing was to be taken for granted.

Gratitude became fluency. Not performative, but intuitive. As natural as a sunrise. As generous as a Good Morning. We were taught to be sincere and grateful—not just for what was given, but for what was yet to come.

This was the devotion cultivated. The providence we inherited. The wait that made space for immaturity to ripen, one simple act of care at a time.

Have you connected the relationship between Waiting and Worthiness?

My earliest memories of waiting as an enthusiastic pursuit and a spiritual practice were celebrated each year in the sacred halls of the neighborhood Anglican Church with a tradition called Harvest Sunday. Although hosted by clergy, it wasn't limited to robes or rituals; it was an open house for the community.

On this day, Patience was not abstract—it was tangible, edible, relatable; it was palpable.

The church converted into a sanctuary of earthly blessings. Ground provisions spread across altars like offerings of glory. Sugarcane, cassava, pumpkins, sweet potatoes, bananas, wild fruits, and leafy greens—all accompanied by the laughter and conversations of those who brought them.

Young minds didn't yet understand liturgy, but they understood longing. The oohs and awes—rising from simmering pots and the rustling of corn husks—were the smells of love that filled us with anticipation. The deliciousness of coconut rice and peas preached its own gospel. The texture of roasted sweet potatoes spoke of a back-bending toil. We weren't taught patience—we tasted it.

The sugar cakes and coconut-filled tarts satisfied the senses with a sweet Amen!

The seasons catechized us long before formal doctrine. Waiting became destined for Good Things. Food became Worship. And Devotion—a daily act of Noticing and Nurturing. Offering—was paid forward into the hearts and consciousness of future generations.

Harvest Sunday was more than a celebration. It was a metaphor for "there is a time and place for everything."

Time to Prepare. Time to Sow. Time for Care. Time to Reap.

Time to Share.

Abundance was a Shared Virtue, where every bite was a hallelujah!

Your attention span was nurtured in accordance with Nature's plan.

Practical. Hands-on. Involved.

Nowadays, Waiting has been replaced by grab-and-go and quick-and-easy options. We unbox, stream, scroll, and receive—all at speeds that disrupt our naturally developed sensory awareness.

The hunger that taught us restraint is now satisfied before it even develops. The 'want it now—get it now—have it now' mindset isn't just quick—it's superficial. And in that rush, Patience is quietly banished.

Where Harvest Sunday used to represent a treasured family tradition—from planting to hard work to sharing a communal feast—it now risks becoming just a story of the good old days.

An event on the calendar. A photo opportunity. A disconnection.

A hashtag, maybe?

What was once grounded in commitment, effort, observatory learning, and weathered through storms of uncertainty is now hurriedly showcased without context. Without the full sensory experience.

We no longer taste the sun in our fruit. We no longer feel the ache in the soil's delay. We eat gluttonously, ravenously, unprepared, and unripe.

We must stop, pause, and taste the food.

Good things are not limited by the ticking clock or rushed by the hurried breath of modern life. They are timelessly rooted in rituals and traditions of devotion. They are not just results—they are offerings that nourish more than appetite—they feed memories, enrich culture, and foster reciprocity.

A universal palate, a shared plate.

A giving spirit aligns with nature's circadian rhythm. Being touched by a devotee's hand is an act of kindness. And to sit and feast in harvest is a reminder that abundance is never the work of one alone.

It's in conjunction with....

Patience was more than a lesson—it was the living truth. Waiting wasn't because you were unready; it was shaping you to be prepared, to be ready.

Good things, when grown in the sunlight of Care and the rainfall of Grace, and rest in the Still of Night, have no expiration date.

They Multiply. They Revive. They Restore.

So, when we talk about "Good Things," we refer to a legacy of spirit, soil, and service.

A gift passed from hand to hand, season to season, heart to soul.

A Spiritual Harvest.

God's Gift.

Your Self-worthiness.

Good Things are an Offering that comes to those who have waited, "with Unconditional Love."

Beneath the soil of Stillness, something stirs—not loudly, but faithfully.

Good things.

Fifth

Casualty of Impatience

"Self-Betrayal"

Forget the Soul.

Look.

Look at the medallions of validation. Golden. Shiny. What would I not do to win? To achieve status? To get on the podium?

Hooked.

Dopamine Overdrive.

This rewiring of the brain's reward system is a craving for instant gratification.

Likes, shares, and notifications trigger erratic surges similar to those caused by performance-enhancing hacks, shrinking the integrity of the attention span. The constant scrolling and digital snacking fragment the ability to stay focused, worsening our cognitive functionality.

That we know, but who cares?

The days when a picture was worth a thousand words are long gone and have now been minimized to a posting, if you're lucky.

The race to nowhere is facing its toughest leg yet—the mental stage. This is where distortion kicks in.

Comparison is enabled.

Self-judgment drains the battery. And FOMO?

For those unfamiliar with the jargon—a 'Fear of Missing Out.' That's right. When did that become a thing? Pardon the rhetoric.

Constant exposure to curated lives—where one creates feelings of inadequacy, envy, and a fear of missing out—leads to anxiety, depression, and a false sense of confidence.

We know all too well how filters and idealized self-images can foster insecurity. While self-betrayal in adults dealing with the shame of competition, the impact on youth is alarmingly different, leaving us with a troubling question of 'where do we go from here?'

Seriously.

As a slandered mind becomes hypervigilant, constantly scanning for social cues, approval, or threats, a state of ongoing mental fatigue begins to develop.

Hardly any spots left for participants in this race; the field is so crowded, as social media withdrawal triggers intermittent anxiety attacks.

Sleep Deprivation. Blue light and late-night scrolling suppress melatonin, impairing sleep quality. And as for the impact on our circadian rhythms? Well, it's been artificialized, as you'd expect.

You've invested so much of your 24-hour window virtual shopping; a sedentary lifestyle has snuck up on you, overshadowing your ability to discern with discretion.

In this digital race, where casual conduct is often stylized and privacy commodified, discretion becomes not just viable—but necessary.

Restraint, the voice of self-awareness, a gentle refusal to be consumed by the algorithmic gaze, has also vanished. Self-indulgence with an undercurrent of depression—suppression—and repression has strengthened to a state of denial.

How did we slip into this food coma from digital snacking?

How do we restore a respect for unseen consequences before it's too late? Revive it so it pauses before acting?

Reassures a healthy conscience before impulse drags you down the road of compulsion?

In a culture obsessed with the illusion of presence, there is a rarer strength. The eloquence of absence. The ability to refrain. To reflect. To discern not in haste, but in stillness.

But even knowing that, you still follow along.

"If the path is clear, you might be blazing someone else's trails."

To whom do I cherish such wisdom?

What are my options? Do I face reality? Or do I continue to feed the soul of boredom?

Going for a casual stroll down to the digital marketplace, the hub of casual shopping, where you can find almost anything.

Casual talk. Casual fun. Casual friends. Casual food. Casual drinks. Casual drugs. Casual sex.

Casual Relationship. Casual everything.

The neon lights of casual entertainment pour through a cracked window. Inside, a crowd gathers—not to connect, but to consume, or perhaps, consummate. The atmosphere pulses with a low-grade vibration of pretense and programmed pleasure, where the language of intimacy has been reduced to emojis, GIFs, and hashtags.

Laughter flows like forbidden syrup—sweet, quick, forgettable. Beneath it, the soul recoils.

Scrolling. Swiping. Browsing. Posting.

Things have started to pick up. In a digital frenzy, scrolling through algorithmic feeds, fingertips stained with artificial coloring, red and blue from overuse.

What once provided a real connection now produces only convenience, inexpensive but nonetheless tempting.

Conversations drift like helium—light, effortless, unanchored.

"Hey," "LOL," "OMG," "Just vibes." Nothing sticks. Nothing lingers.

Empty words.

'Hello' used to carry meaning. Now it's just code.

'How are you?'

Too deep of a prod, just a casual inquiry.

Is this a real connection or just a sensation?

Illusions choreographed by digital auctioneers, competing for your attention. Behind every glance is a transaction. Behind every click is an addiction.

Bonding diminishes to bandwidth. Fellowship turns into followership. Anxiety masquerades profusely as free will.

The scene gets louder. Selfies and content creation increase. Just one image can capture the essence of your story.

Highlights. Short reels driven by dopamine-fueled comparison spark dissatisfaction. The once-valued Human touch, Consideration, and Care now hide behind filters and avatars.

The voice inside barely speaks, suffering beneath the Chaos—Why is everyone in such a rush? What's with all the noise? Why aren't they listening?

Who can I trust?

Atrophied and aching, a soul drained by superficial connections, claws for meaning below the surface of casual chatter.

The evening is in full swing as happiness is on the clock, limited to an hour or two. With an attention span that could hardly see straight, as toxicity ramps up. Short-sighted, bewildered; how did a good time lose its edge so quickly?

Notifications ring like alarms—
URGENT, IMPORTANT, NOW!

The long game? What is that? We no longer plan for seasons or years. We react to flashes, twitching at every ping.

FOMO has become a controlling disorder of its own. But what are we truly afraid of missing out on? What do we imagine awaits on the other side of that scroll, that click, or that quiet moment alone in the crowd?

Are we missing the reminder that we're not enough? Are we running out of time on a wild goose chase? Have we fallen for the naysayers who say that joy is overrated?

Have you accepted anxiety as normal?

There's something inside me that feels wrong. But I have to get back out there. The world needs me, or so I believe.

Back at it again. Casual bites turn into casual nights. Casual play turns into casual stays.

Casual struggles for days.

Struggling to regain my soul. Struggling to attract attention under the pretense of becoming a better version. Struggling to free the soul from its casual barriers—those slow-acting toxins hidden as trends, memes, and faux likes.

The battle is fought silently. Not with swords, but with cool selfies. Not with shields, but with slogans. The Soul, once connected in good conscience, is now a battlefield filled with disposable affirmations and insincere lingo.

We fight for relevance. We're battling for presence. We fight to be seen through the stream.

Is this thriving? Is this creativity?

Apparently, this is content creation.

Discontentment.

Patience, oh patience, where art thou?

Talking to a friend about patience, I admitted, "We can't even wait for the shortcuts to end." And he didn't hesitate. "Yes," he said, "but what's crazier, though, is that we are now shortcutting the shortcuts."

There it is; Even impatience has grown more impatient.

Where is the meaning in these fleeting thrills and digital frills? They shine briefly, attracting attention like moths to a fake flame—but they don't nourish the soul for long. Casualness excites the present moment, but loses gravity with quickness. It affirms the algorithm's intention but doesn't fulfill genuine affection.

Were we made for artificial applause? Or should we praise the Spiritual-Mind-Body warriors, clinging to actuality?

If spirituality is an abstract concept, then let me mold it into a tangible reality.

The mind isn't mechanical, but without understanding, it becomes mechanized. The body isn't unconditional, but without self-awareness, the unconditional becomes conditioned.

The Spirit isn't artificial, but even in casual situations, its presence remains supernatural.

Patience, in this hyper-superficial maze, feels like rebellion—like handwriting in a world of autofill, like silence in a space drowned with sound. It's a race to transcend the very self we haven't yet understood. The one we betrayed. And in doing so, we lose the pulse that gave us purpose.

There are lessons to be learned from the Unnatural Teacher.

Impatience, impatience, impatience—it eats out of unwashed hands. No pause. No grace. No discernment. Just feed the hungry bellies of self-fulfillment.

Like Nature, casualness is a teacher. But it doesn't teach seasons; it teaches speed. It doesn't teach balance; it teaches shortcuts. It doesn't teach gratitude; it leads to compulsion.

The casual voice confidently asserts that our self-worth can be measured.

If 'how many' is your price, then 'how much' is the cost of bidding on your soul?

It teaches Contradiction—Comparison—Chaos. Coping with Conflict. It disregards the Inner Sense.

Here—disillusionment turns into doctrine. We mistake apathy for normalcy. Casual attitudes warp the integrity of Virtue and Values. It hides emptiness behind a facade labeled "Confidence."

And what's the result? We are left soullessly wandering— malnourished in unworthiness, dehydrated in indifference, never realizing that we are Casualties of Impatience.

Casualties of Casualness.

We are now taught to rush, not to revere. To broadcast, not to listen. To perform, not to be present. This is not just a cultural trend—it's a spiritual bend.

It has its own gospel—a Gospel of Can't Wait.

Casually speaking, a shallow language of hurry without depth—a dialect born of unawareness.

We say, "Can't wait to grow up." "Can't wait to finish school." "Can't wait to find a good job." "Can't wait to marry." "Can't wait to be healthy."

While being sick of ourselves.

"Can't wait to feel better."

What's the end goal? Where are we headed?

This isn't just premature anticipation—it's a depletion of the inner sense.

"Can't wait" no longer shows excitement.

Running out of Faith,

"Can't wait to go to heaven."

Unawareness teaches us to run from Commitment before it develops. To abandon Joy before it takes hold. To skim across Life like a stone hurled across deep water—never sinking, never staying—just shimmering.

In this state, we disconnect not only from time but also from truth. The soul no longer learns; it just repeats. And the heart becomes something that paces, not something that feels.

To regain Awareness, we must slow down speech, reduce our words, lengthen the silence, and reintroduce Waiting, not as Control—but as Participation.

To unlearn "can't wait," we need to relearn "I'm here." To unlearn "casual fate," we need to relearn "Be still."

And Patience as a Promise, in this endless state of "casualness," we find ourselves tangled—not timelessly, but in contradiction, rotting beneath the urgency. We crave presence yet run from pause. We long for meaning while skipping over depth.

The fractured soul: a Contradiction between desire and discipline.

Are we supposed to sit soullessly, as a Casualty of Impatience, expected to be taken seriously? Or is this the moment when the Timeless

Wonder invites us to 'See the Truth in Contradiction?'

A betrayal of self: Going against one's own core Values and Virtues, and Truth, to gain unwarranted approval, often resulting in a disconnection. Feelings of guilt.

Fragmented.

Ignoring the Innocence of the Inner Sense.

How does one regain realignment?

As one rises from the monotonous energy of casualness, we begin to listen—not to the noise of contradiction, but to the whisper beneath it.

Toward redemption.

Sixth

Seeing the Truth in Contradiction

"Self-Redemption"

As we go through the escalating stages of the Relationship Challenge, the difficulty doesn't just rise—it sharpens. The path becomes narrower, the stakes grow deeper, and the illusions become louder. And in the fog of apathy, contradiction turns into chicanery.

A mind game.

It offers simplicity without truth and full membership into the comfort zone.

One doesn't have to dig very deep or look very far to find contradiction—we are immersed in it. It fills our thoughts, influences our actions, and echoes across land and sea. It headlines news, controls institutions, shapes stories, and harms communities.

Its digitization has upped the ante, strengthening the bandwidth of chaos, conflict, and condescension; from interruption to disruptions, they become habits. The social order is not just fractured—it's combustible.

Highly imitable.

We consume its fiery dissonance like it were music, inappropriate to the masses but catchy.

But contradiction cannot be the soundtrack of a life well-lived. To heal it, we must first recognize how ingrained in our choices it is. And, with patience, begin the meditation. Chanting integrity over style, truth over charm, harmony over imitation.

This hits close to home for me. I don't know about you, but I have a disdain for hypocrisy. Mine, of course. Yours concerns me, but mine rattles the Soul.

It's easily spotted.

Very detectable by the average eye, and its fickle roots are traceable.

It was time for a wellness check.

I had fallen in love with health. Sounds weird. I know. And like most people who caught the bug, the physical transformation drew a lot of attention. I had put my lifestyle through the wringer by self-evaluating my life choices and became more highly aware of them. I went on a diet cleanse, a detox, along with an intense exercise program, which resulted in immediate weight loss.

It was significant—about 25 pounds, four belt notches down.

I felt fantastic—so much so that I scheduled an early appointment with my doctor. I remember when my doctor first entered the room and saw me. She was amazed by my overall results and physical transformation. Man, she cheered me on!

While I was there, feeling full of myself, after I had gotten a stellar report card, she asked me a couple of questions that would inevitably change the trajectory of my life.

She asked me, "If health is so important to you, why do you smoke?" "And how often do you drink, by the way?" Talk about raining on someone's parade.

She told me, "You need to quit smoking and drinking."

I felt as if I was pushed up against the wall of hypocrisy. I was overwhelmed by the sudden clash of contradiction.

After pressing me, right then and there, I said, "Okay, I'll quit smoking cigars." As for drinking, it was still one of my favorite pastimes and wasn't ready to part ways just yet. I needed more time. She was pleased with the compromise, but I must tell you, I left that appointment with a clean bill of health and a guilty conscience.

I remembered gathering the gang and telling them we had a big night to celebrate. When I shared the big news, "This is my last cigar," a twenty-year streak. I wasn't surprised by the disbelief, sarcasm, or pushback. No one saw it coming, not even me. Yep. It was as simple as that. I'll skip the rest of the story.

Over the years, I gradually followed my doctor's advice and left the drinking behind altogether.

If health were that important, why was I toxifying and intoxicating myself?

Words that stung deep enough for me to act.

This is a critical part of the Relationship Challenge: facing the Truth and eliminating Contradiction.

With the incredible advancements in science and medicine and with the convenience of information at our disposal, it didn't necessarily translate into good health. It highlighted the difference between knowledge and knowing. Knowledge doesn't guarantee action; knowing does.

It revealed to me the power of words.

While we tend to explore the psychological and physiological aspects of health—both brimming with contradictions—the coldness in our speech, the casual cruelty hidden behind authority, and the double meanings and double standards require us to start there.

The implications of our words.

The mixed signals.

Take, for example, "Adult behavior," we say, as if indulgence were maturity. As if profanity, secrecy, and recklessness were markers of adulthood. We assign grown-up status not through virtue but through vice—what one consumes, what one conceals, and what one gets away with.

So we ask: What does it mean to be an adult? Not as a provocation, but in all sincerity. The answer should not depend on legality or lifestyle, but on intentionality.

Adulthood is not a license—it is a responsibility. It is a state of self-awareness where tone becomes a tool for understanding, and language reflects the soul. When words lose their sweetness, actions follow. And in that gap between what we say and what we mean, contradiction is sanctified.

We speak to adolescents with two tongues. One that urges discipline and the other that decorates dysfunction as maturity. We label profanity as adult language, obscenity as adult material, and indulgence as adult behavior. We brand alcohol as adult beverages, infidelity as adultery, and recklessness as grown-up choices. But then we turn to the youth and say, Behave maturely.

These messages do not educate—they confuse. They create uncertainty about what it means to grow, to lead, to become. Adolescents imitate not the wisdom of adulthood, but its contradictions. And when that imitation turns into misconduct, we ask, "Where is the adult in the room?"

The question is not rhetorical—it is spiritual. To be the adult in the room is to embody consistency. To carry integrity not just in moments of crisis, but in daily tone, choices, and language.

It's a common courtesy.

We must redefine adulthood not by indulgence, but by a ripening of the fruits of our labor. Because if our version of adulthood is unworthy of imitation, then we've handed the next generation not a path, but a paradox.

For years, I kept a small prayer, framed. One given to me by a friend. It always seemed to find the right moment to speak to those in need, including myself. It read, "Lord, make my words as sweet as honey, for one day I may have to eat them."

The Truth of Contradiction.

What is Maturity? Doesn't it mean healthy?

Shall we clarify its definition?

Ripeness.

Timeliness.

In essence, maturity originally meant the moment when something is ready—fully formed, complete, and capable of fulfilling its purpose. Whether it's fruit on a tree, a soul in reflection, or a bond reaching its due date, the word conveys a sense of timing and transformation.

Good health. Good conscience. Pure goodness.

To eliminate contradiction is to understand the integral nature of health. So much depends on this. Just looking at its etymological roots alone as referenced earlier, the word 'health' means whole, sane, or holy.

If Contradiction pulls us apart, then Maturity, at its core, welcomes us back into wholeness. It's not about age or authority—it's about alignment. About waking each day with a Good Conscience, moving with Sound-minded Grace, and living from a place of Goodness.

Innocence.

Maturity is a ripeness, not merely a social standing. It edifies a dedication to Health—Good Health, not only the measurable, but also the spiritual.

When we say someone is "whole," we don't mean perfect—we mean Integrated.

Indivisible.

Present.

A being whose actions match their convictions, whose tone uplifts rather than confuses, whose life spills harmony.

Seeing the Truth in Contradiction is not a scolding—it's Redemption. A return to wholeness that makes room for both strength and softness. And in this space, Maturity blossoms—not as duty, but as Readiness.

Just as we've explored Order by understanding Disorder, we can similarly examine maturity and health by asking: What is immaturity?

Is it not unhealthy?

There is an etymological kinship between Health, Patient, and Honesty.

Health is not just the absence of dis-ease—it's the ease with which a person lives. Its roots go back to 'heal,' meaning whole, sound, of good omen.

But healing requires patience. 'To endure'—not just in suffering, but with humility.
And honesty, though etched on a different branch of language, becomes healing's gatekeeper. You cannot heal what you refuse to name. You cannot mature where you won't reflect.

Together, this constellation forms a Deeper Truth: that healing is not just a choice—it is a Spiritual Practice. It is being honest enough to see what hurts, and patient enough to trust what works.

Your Health matters. Your words matter.

"Lord, make my words as sweet as honey, for one day I may have to eat them."

In those words, lie the aspiration to live contradiction-free—not perfect, but with equanimity. A life where speech and spirit walk hand in hand. Where tone uplifts, conduct reflects care, and devotion guides posture.

Speaking truthfully and being wholesome means offering the self—not just to God, but also to those we encounter.

And so, the healing persists, not through grand gestures but in every word that echoes the inner voice.

In truth, this prayer is more than a preview of scripture; it is Maturity.

It's Health.

It is Spirituality.

An Adulthood worth passing on. One without Contradiction.

Contradiction is not just confusion—it's the echo of a deeper harmony waiting to be heard. The truth, when seen through it, is not less clear—it is more whole.

Seventh

Spirits to Spiritual

"Self-Realization"

It wasn't the meeting that unraveled me—it was the moment before I spoke.

The introduction.

The rising swell within.

An unrehearsed ritual I'd executed a countless number of times. But on this day, as I opened my mouth to speak, a thunderous pounding surged in the chest—not nervousness, but a thud. Anxiety didn't tap politely; it tried to tear through skin and bone, desperate to escape.

The room, formal and professional, became a coliseum. All eyes on me. It felt like every second stretched like slow motion under a spotlight of judgment.

My voice cracked, betrayed by the shortness of breath. Hands shook as if auditioning for surrender. The perspiration wasn't visible, but it was felt—hot under the collar.

Invasive.

Mortifying.

My body became a transcript of contradiction. Poised yet petrified. Successful, yet apprehensive.

It was a Panic Attack.

An informant.

A reckoning.

It came not as retribution, but as a rescue. Emerging from the rubble and the aftermath of years and years of ignorance and neglect. The inner voice had had enough.

It was instructive.

It said, "There is no time like the present."

"You know deep down what's at the root of these attacks. You cannot hide from yourself any longer."

Due diligence wasn't a professional obligation—it was personal. I had to turn inward to confront the apprehension. To finally surrender to the obedience beneath the thunder.

This is not the story of one who lost control. It's the story of being saved from the illusion of being in control.

I had built a life, yes—a good one. One that read: "From dishwasher to director." But even then, a good reputation can only mask the anxiety for so long. Deep inside, something lassoed me from premonition.

On the surface, shyness wasn't just social awkwardness I hid behind; it was the early language of my inner feelings—fragile and pure. It taught me to listen more than speak, to pay attention to tone more than take words at face value.

Conventional wisdom says you have to conquer this fear. But this? This isn't a dragon to slay. It's a sea to swim. Unearthing wisdom doesn't come with a diploma or applause—it comes with the unsettling honesty of realizing you've betrayed your own soul.

This wasn't a gut feeling. It wasn't even intuition. It was an intervention. A call so powerful that no amount of spirits could drown it.

I tried, Lord knows I tried to wash it down, laugh it off, and push it aside. But it waited. Then, there was silence—it didn't shame me. It embraced me. Then, it handed me a pen.

It asked me to write down what I was afraid of.

I'd spent years chasing composure, thinking wholeness was about getting it all right. But fear has a way of cracking that illusion wide open. The fright wasn't insecurity—it was wisdom, trying to speak through my chest.

The pain?

That was the messenger asking, 'Will you finally listen?'

I was ready.

I did.

Not by fixing, but by honoring what I was feeling. Not by pretending, but by writing. I realized that innocence hadn't abandoned me—it had simply grown tired of waiting to be chosen.

What surprised me most on this journey wasn't that others saw themselves in me. It was how I saw myself in them—and I finally liked what I saw. That little tremble in someone's voice, that guarded smile, that unsure answer when asked "How are you?"—I knew it all too well. And I wanted them to know. You don't have to be perfect to be worthy.

You just have to be real.

Being yourself isn't risky. It's revolutionary.

And in a lifetime of roles, achievements, and milestones, it turns out that the coolest thing I've ever done was just that... to be me.

In reflection, they tried to call it enlightenment—a phase. They said, I'd change. But the truth is—it was a calling.

Not a hunch. Not instinct. Not even a gut feeling.

It grew louder.

Deeper.

Out of body.

Spiritual.

Whether dulled by drinks or numbed by noise—whether hidden behind applause or lost in it—I learned: there was no bottle big enough, no indulgence rich enough, no philosophy mind-bending enough to quiet the voice that said, "just be you."

This inner voice wasn't asking for attention. It ascended to a higher level of self-awareness.

I spent years perfecting subtitles for a book that remained unnamed. Unread. Lost in social misappropriation, where comfort without clarity becomes a disguise. And eventually, that camouflage reflected who I had become.

Wisdom once said, "You can't fool Spirit."

"Spirit knows."

It knows when you're dodging, even when you don't. It waits, dormant, whilst you are asleep.

The ecdysis of acceptance wasn't loud. It was slow and steady. Like a wind chime drifting quietly, becoming clearer until every echo of doubt was finally overshadowed by redemption.

This is where spiritual living starts—not with perfection, but with questions. Not with answers, but through observation.

Was this a call to serve? And if so, in service of what? In service of whom?

In service of Truth? In service of Health? In service of Love? A range of possibilities awaited.

Spiritual—beyond definition and description. Not a declaration, not a proclamation, not a volume level.

It is the courage to listen when the world shouts. The bold humility to change even when ego resists. And the persistent pursuit of order, especially when contradiction tempts you to return to the comforts of the old self.

Listen... and solitude becomes Truth. Be Still... and hope finds a home in others. Live with Grace... and condemnation loses its grip. Not because you've vanquished it, but because Faith vanished it.

This is what the Spirit knows. This is what the Soul remembers.

When self-doubt veils your clarity... listen deeper.

If impatience trespasses on your stillness... reclaim your balance. Do not be discouraged.

To whom much is given, much is expected—but remember, the strength to carry it isn't just a gift; it's a baton.

Broad shoulders are not bought. They're built—in Pain, in Practice, in Presence.

Work through the Challenge. Don't run from the tremor. Like my Panic Attack, it came not to destroy me—but to deliver a message:

"From dishwasher to director brought great pride, but spirits to spiritual healed inside."

This redemption is Self-Realization.

Eighth

Nature's Embrace

"Self-Renewal"

I did not perform well in school. Grades fluctuated.

One year was super, another mediocre. The cycle continued throughout my school years.

No one said whether I was a good student or not. The teachers were consistent in calling it like they saw it.

"Uninterested," they said I was. "Room for improvement," they said, I have.

Nothing too harsh, nothing great.

Whether intentional or not, I was very selective about what I retained. To this day, certain subjects and topics have stayed with me.

There was a strong gravitational pull toward Nature. I remembered learning about Photosynthesis. I don't recall my age or what grade I was in, but I remember the subject matter as if it were tattooed on the sleeve of my awareness.

The Sun.

The symbiotic relationship between plants, animals, and us

human beings. It was science, but for me, it felt like an enlightenment. It was like the first time I saw a firefly. How dare you tell me magic isn't real?

How could these rays of sunlight turn into this green, energetic source filled with vitamins and nutrients called chlorophyll? How are these plants inhaling the carbon dioxide flowing from my diaphragm?

Their needs are ours, just as ours are theirs.

The cycle of interdependency fascinated me, as I learned about Nature's brilliance of turning radiance into sustenance.

Photosynthesis.

The process plants use to convert sunlight, carbon dioxide, and water into glucose (a type of sugar they use for energy) and oxygen (which they release into the air for you, animals, and me).

Why? So that we can live with vitality.

Exploring synchronicity in relationship, both literally and figuratively, thank God that I haven't lost touch with Nature—the connection. It still lives with vigor within me.

What is vibrant living without it?

This may seem strange for some, but I also had a thing for earthworms, long before uncovering their invaluable servitude to a fertile land.

When I was little, I loved digging my hands into the soil, especially when it was time to pull carrots, potatoes, and peanuts. I chomped at the bit each time, eager and couldn't wait to taste the carrots. It was like a reveal, an unboxing.

Some were scrawny and stringy, while others were jumbo in size. The soil was rich, filled with earthworms, a sign of microbial activity.

You didn't even wash the carrots back then; you crunched on them like the rabbits did. Fresh from the ground, dusted off to perfection.

Have you tried eating raw potatoes? You must give it a go. It surprises a curious tongue. There was the duopoly of the nut family—the cashews, known to us as cherry seeds, and the peanuts, representing heaven and hell—well, not quite, but one growing below the ground and the other above, both providing nutrients that sustained us throughout most of the day.

The earthworms—laborers of love with more purpose than one could imagine.

The soil today, chemically laced for mass production or unpreserved, has driven the earthworms into extinction, and with that, we're feeding off a land like AstroTurf for nutrition.

Convenient.

Expedient.

Infertile.

Let's get back to the salt of the earth—the earthworms. These little buggers. What do they really do?

The story goes that beneath the surface of every thriving garden, a mystical underworld unfolds—crafted not by machinery or humans, but by earthworms and their insect friends.

These unheralded laborers embody Nature's embrace.

Aerating the soil through burrowing that breathes life into the land. Their tunnels create vital pathways for water and air, loosening compacted earth and inviting roots to deepen in search of nourishment.

As they move and feed, earthworms convert organic matter into castings rich in nitrogen, phosphorus, and microbial vitality—turning decay into abundance. Their movements create the structural foundation of healthy soil, binding particles into porous aggregates that retain moisture and prevent erosion.

In their simplicity, they model harmony—unseen yet indispensable, humble with necessity.

Together, these creatures choreograph a symphony of renewal that transcends biology—spiritual, relational, and symbolic.

To honor the soil is to honor these treasured bonds.

In the choreography of these tiny architects, we glimpse the blueprint of connection. Every particle, wingbeat, and worm cast is a call to remember that true renewal begins beneath.

As the hummingbird teaches us to be still, even in full motion, the earthworms, their suppleness and ease remind us that fertility is a partnership.

The Soil—the Inner Sense, for it to be fertile with innocence, one must be receptive to the lessons in the Lightness of Dark.

In the same soil, where earthworms labor unseen, the hummingbird hovers—a flash of iridescence, a whisper of wonder, hoping to be seen.

Where the worm teaches us patience and depth, the hummingbird counters with agility, duty, and joyfully living in the now. Though delicate in stature, the hummingbird endures the storm. It migrates vast distances, defying its size. It reminds us that strength is not always loud—it is reserved for the task at hand.

Their rapid wingbeats and nectar-seeking dance teach us to savor sweetness without clinging.

Devotion unquestioned; they return to the same flowers, the same feeders, day after day. This ritual is not habit—it's remembrance. A hummingbird's loyalty to nourishment mirrors our spiritual need for consistency in prayer, meditation, and in retreat.

As messengers of hope, across cultures, hummingbirds are seen as bearers of joy, healing, and ancestral whispers. Their appearance often signals renewal, reminding us that beauty can arrive in the blink of a wing.

The Worm Below, The Bird Above: together, the earthworm and the hummingbird form a sacred bond. The worm aerates the soil, unseen but essential, while the hummingbird pollinates the air, fleeting but aware.

One moves through darkness to feed the roots. The other dances in light to feed the bloom. Both are devoted. Both are necessary. Renewal, then, is not just reconnection—it is coexistence across realms, cultures—signified Nature's Grace.

To betray Nature is to betray the very breath that animates us. She is inseparable to soul-worthiness—soulful despite her wrath; she is source to all forms of life, energy fueling the land.

In our heightened impatient demand, the soil we refuse to touch, the flower we fail to notice, the ocean we neglect to hear—they are not just ornaments, they are teaching us to be austere.

When we disconnect, we not only lose green energy—we lose green virtues: patience, reverence, reciprocity.

We lose Vitality.

What legacy can stand if its roots are severed from the land? What protection endures if the mother's heart is abandoned?

When nature is honored as both mirror and mentor, it awakens dormant faculties within us. Not just cognition, but communion. It doesn't speak in linear propositions—it gestures, it pulses, it reflects. Observation becomes awareness, not just skill.

And that imbalance, disconnection—that tilt toward analysis over intuition—feels like a spiritual amnesia. Left-brain dominance often values control, segmentation, and efficiency. But nature isn't segmented—it's cyclical, relational, improvisational. When we ignore it, we risk severing ourselves from the teachings of dusk, dew, and decay.

One must establish a "spiritual nucleus" like that of fireflies—bioluminescent metaphors for inner illumination.

We've mistaken information for wisdom, and in doing so, we've dulled our senses to Beauty, to Suffering, to Spirit. This is the atrophy—not just the body, not just the intellect, but of the soul.

Therefore, we retreat. Not with shame, but with urgency. To touch the soil again. To look a hummingbird in the eye. To walk barefoot on the land.

To offer devotion not through rhetoric, but through renewal. Because when one says that God is within, the echo is clear. You are Nature. And to love God rightly is to conserve what sustains us.

To Preserve Beauty before it fades.

It's unforgiving not to heal what you've hurt. It is soul-satisfying to sing a redemption song where silence has taken root.

Nature's Embrace is still open. To step into it is not a choice; choosing to neglect it, abandon it, is.

The World is in desperate need of a Retreat.

Retreat isn't an escape—it's a Time for Recalibration.

In the dissonance of repetition and casualness, the soul becomes mechanical, forgetting how to feel, how to listen. But beneath that static lies a silent revolution: Stillness, untouched by time.

When true connection is lost, the soul begins to mimic that which was created to mimic us, technology—looping tiresomely, numbed by repetition—a Retreat is Intervention.

Listen to Inner Wisdom.

Pause with Intention.

To return to Beauty is to inhale creation's first breath again and again and again.

There, among trees that do not hurry and birds that do not posture, we might just remember that Truth is not manufactured.

It is nurtured.

It enriches the Soil, reinvigorates the Spirit, it glimmers in the wings of a hummingbird, and labors in the worms at toil.

What would you give for Nature's Embrace? Where would you go in Retreat?

Nineth

The Promise

"Self-Consciousness"

Whether stuck at the crossroads or caught in the crosshairs of Relationship—Life, one begins not with instruction, but with inquisition—an entry point to a language spoken long before words, the Innocence of the Inner Sense.

This is not weakness; it's an imposition, insistent on finding answers to the ultimate question.

A question that lingers like a gateway drug to Truth.

It's the honesty we held before identity was taught to perform. It's the language the soul still speaks, with an unvarnished eloquence and beauty.

It's happiness. It's joy. It's laughter.

It is devilishly complex.

And simplistically, pure.

It's a realization.

Welcome to—The Relationship Challenge.

The Challenge isn't just a framework. It's the universal dialect of human beings—a living mirror held up to our instincts, our longings, our wounds. It asks, not in certainty but in curiosity, what we mean when we say connection, what we risk when we say love, what we hope for in surrendering to wisdom.

Each era—from post-machinery to electrification, computerization, and AI—addresses the moment differently. But beneath the surface, the Human Condition renders the same.

Tender. Unpredictable. Uncertain.

Challenged. Problematic. Tension.

Jealous. Envious. Low vibration.

Guilt. Resentful. Redemption

Healed. Free.

Liberation.

A shared commonality threads the soul of everyone, requiring a care that timelessly spells devotion.

It demands Patience, not because growth is slow, but because patience is the maturation of expectation. And in today's lay of the land—overrun by speed, overstimulated by sensationalism—our inner gardener must be more attuned than ever to meet the challenge of restoration.

Hence, meditation.

Yet even here, amidst the elemental perplexity that is the digital footprint, the soil remains fertile in faith, ready to be nurtured with intention.

Wherever innocence looms, truth is possible. Wherever vulnerability is, awareness flows. Whenever Relationship is questioned with dignity, the soul fondly remembers.

The Relationship Challenge—a conscious-unconscious wave breaking into dialogue. How else is one to know who they are—how they'd become?

Who would've thought that a little over two decades ago, conceptualizing the word RELATIONSHIPS into a behavioral alphabet for relational inquiry would revive a reconnection—with others, yes, but most importantly, within oneself.

This is not a test—it is a testimony.

The Challenge began with a word we all know, often feared, and sometimes revered: RELATIONSHIPS.

What happens when we let this word breathe, more letters arrive. When it teaches rather than commands? When we listened to its inference, instead of reacting to its indifference?

When we trusted its inner sense, not its indulgence.

Across cultures, creeds, and contradictions, I discovered a unifying thread. When people are given the opportunity to reflect openly, privately, or confidentially, they return to basic universal principles. Principles of agreeance that cut through the core aspects of our shared human experience.

Patience. Respect. Enthusiasm. Sharing. Openness. Listening. Trust. Honesty. Individuality. Inspiration. The ingredients we seek externally, that have always been inherently within us.

This challenge became a mirror—an open question—an inquiry—not of judgment, but of a readiness to learn and grow.

What's beautiful about its reveal is how it enlivened understanding. It was amazing to see how, with the right ambiance, tone, and energy, people spoke enthusiastically.

That ambiance: 'I don't know,' gave way to a knowing that sat waiting for its mention.

It felt like a ritual, unrehearsed and unpracticed—but somehow, accommodating. It was like letting fresh air into a muggy room.

Some inhaled realization, while others exhaled redemption.

I saw how our shared human truths unhooked the grips of fear. Loosened the reins of a prideful reputation and softened the tone of biases and beliefs. It affirmed that on our alternative life paths, we each carry some of the same mosaic: curiosity, vulnerability, longing, and dignity.

Time and again, it felt like unwriting a love story.

Intrigued, the inquisition had remarkable positive energy, and even though no one I had spoken to shared the same answers as I did, it funneled the attention into focus.

It showed that although our upbringing and ways of expressing ourselves are different, the core things we want in a relationship—empathy, compassion, and understanding—all have universal appeal.

That, in itself, brought immense self-satisfaction, but it was the self-discovery that liberated the anxiety.

This by no means meant that the Relationship Challenge for all was smooth sailing. While there was a tendency to tackle the challenge with aspirational fervor, it might have created a blind spot at times. There was always this little twist. Like a curveball. No one expected the obvious to lie so nonchalantly in plain sight.

The obvious was ANGER. Yes, the mighty Anger!

That's the seismic answer to the question. One that brought disbelief to a standstill and delivered fear from belief.

Everyone recognizes anger, yet rarely names it as foundational. I suppose aspirational thinking often sanitizes reality. We want to be ideal, but we forget that Relationship—real, messy, transformative Relationship—requires a confrontation with the shadow.

Pivotal, I might add.

But here was where wisdom gracefully stepped in; the deep-seated anger, when acknowledged, becomes an unbelievable teacher. Not timeless like humility, but a momentary reflection of what must change, what must be voiced, what must be felt in order to evolve.

It's bounded, yes—but with Patience, it can unlock the truth of the timeless.

That was the pearl of the jewels we uncovered. And for those who struggled to uncover it, it sits as anxiety, in waiting.

How has 'A Dozen Roses' flowered since its publication? Knowing that Love is the answer, these are questions to ponder.

(Feel free to respond in writing, or in meditation.)

R – Respect: What grounds your intentions in dignity and regard?

E – Enthusiasm: What lifts your spirit into joyful participation?

L – Listening: When was the last time you truly heard without interruption?

A – Anger: What truth has your anxiety been trying to express?

T – Trust: Where have you placed your worthiness, and what did it reveal?

I – Individuality: How do you honor your indivisibility without apology?

O – Openness: What does vulnerability create in your life?

N – Nurturing: What habits of care secure your evolving?

S – Sharing: What have you offered freely, without reciprocation?

H – Honesty: How do you face the truth even when it's uncomfortable?

I – Inspiration: What ignites your vision or calls your soul forward?

P – Patience: When was the last time you waited long enough for something real to flower?

S – Successful: If you could redefine "success" to align with Purpose, what would it be, and when would you begin?

Your answers point to the impediments of change. Your change is to honor the Innocence of the Inner Sense. Only you can hear what it's saying, feel what it's expressing.

Be Patient.

Let your questions blossom.

Trust will bloom.

But in the end, those seeds of innocence require your undivided attention.

May this challenge inspire a shift in consciousness.

Meeting you, wherever you are.

What we know often masks what we feel. What we understand can be misunderstood by a desire to reveal.

But if you understand that 'Patience' is not finite, but is a seeker of understanding, you'll see The Relationship Challenge, not as a one-time quiz, but a living inquiry, moment by moment. An innocent question asked again and again: What does it mean to connect deeply? Whom do I bring to Relationship—my curated version, or my presence?

It asks: Can I be sincere without pretense, and real without permission?

These are not quick and easy resolutions; these are days and nights of timeless breaths, and inquisition.

Take a moment—to pause. To remember that the Inner Sense isn't gone—it's waiting. And in remembering, we reclaim it—not as childlike, but Soul-wise.

And with that, we walk on, not toward the next chapter, but deeper into self-consciousness.

Unbroken. Unfazed. Unafraid.

The Relationship Challenge is essentially a Promise to nurture Health. A Promise to never stop reading the Book of Life. A Promise to edify Gratitude.

And to do so with PATIENCE.

Tenfold

A Meditative Heart

"Selfless"

With a pedigree of exceptionalism, we often boast about how far we've come. Modernization, technology, and artificial intelligence stand as symbols of achievements at the peak of invention. Such progress. Such a revolution. Increasing numbers of emerging markets, more and more competition.

What I am challenging is our state of evolution. Knowing what human beings were capable of centuries ago, without the advancements we enjoy today.

You've heard the term 'ancient wisdom' and it's undoubtedly not evoking time, but the timeless.

Have you ever considered the patience and wisdom of the meditative souls that brought us the alphabet? What communication must have felt like. A new awareness, a new potentiality, shaping consciousness, bringing the world together through linguistic precision, one symbol, one word, one sentence at a time.

The grammatical formulas. The pronunciation. The definitions with their singular and multiple meanings.

The trials and triumphs.

Writing. Scripting. Essaying. Documenting. Storytelling.

Could you imagine going from illiteracy to literacy? Can you imagine the focus and commitment and brilliance and the evolved state of consciousness from the early days of the Babylonians, the Phoenicians, the Greeks, and the Latin, an endeavor transcribed into the English language and multiple other interpretations?

Imagine the Babylonian scribe, pressing wedge-shaped marks into clay—each stroke a prayer to order, to permanence.

The Phoenician merchant, etching symbols onto papyrus, carrying language across seas like precious cargo.

The Greek philosopher, shaping logic and poetry with vowels that gave breath to thought.

The Latin monk, transcribing texts by candlelight, preserving the soul of civilization through ink and devotion.

This wasn't just literacy—it was illumination.

What if the alphabet itself were a metaphor for spiritual rebirth?

A for Awareness

B for Balance

C for Care

...each letter a virtue, a threshold, a step in the pilgrimage from chaos to order.

As if that wasn't mind-blowing enough, what about the meditative hearts, the creators of Math? A number system without which there is no currency, no formula, no codes, no robotics, no AI, as we know them today.

From Intuition to Abstraction.

Prehistoric humans used tally marks on bones and cave walls—like the Ishango bone in Africa—to track lunar cycles and resources.

These early marks weren't just practical—they were ritualistic, tied to survival, intuition, and awareness.

Babylonian Brilliance.

The Babylonians developed a base-60
system over 5,000 years ago, which still shapes
how we measure time and angles.

5,000 years ago!!

W.O.W.

Their math was deeply tied to astronomy,
suggesting a contemplative relationship with the
heavens.

Indian Enlightenment.

Ancient Indian mathematicians introduced
the decimal system and the concept of zero—a
philosophical and mathematical revolution.

Thinkers
like Aryabhata and Brahmagupta weren't just
solving equations—they were
exploring infinity, emptiness, and cosmic order.

Meditation in Motion

Mathematics emerged
from stillness, observation, and pattern
recognition—qualities deeply aligned with
meditation.

The act of counting, measuring, and calculating
is a form of devotional focus, a way to
bring order to chaos, form to void.

Centuries ago, human beings were far more evolved beyond scales unimaginable. Why? Because they meditated—not in silence alone, but inherently in Pursuit of Order. Of Harmony. Of Balance.

Fulfilling a need. Enshrining an observation. A timeless approach to Nature.

Just the thought alone befuddles me. The heightened state of awareness peaked, leading to the invention of the Timeless Systems. Ones that've withstood the test of time, years and years, and centuries later.

I am chalking it up to the Power of Meditation.

In conversations with friends, particularly discussing pressing matters, I've often said to them: "Meditate on it."

It catches them off guard. I never defined it or said what it was. But intuitively, it spoke to something within them; they knew.

There is an understanding.

It inspired a lightness. Wonderment. A pause.

Meditation has shaped cultures, systems, and other-worldly affairs as we know them. But beyond the systematic, have we considered its physiological effects? Its psychological dimension? Its spiritual resonance?

What does meditation mean in conjunction with our health?

Science has its say. But what do you say?

Within the infinite Nature of Stillness, what possibilities lie ahead?

What is the next great pursuit that will lift the soul out of atrophy for generations and generations to come?

Would you meditate on it?

I am.

Years ago, I decided to take on something much bigger than myself: "The Relationship Challenge."

Just like the inventors of linguistics and mathematics saw a need, can we create a non-systematic approach that brings Order to Relationships?

For me, this merited an inquisition.

This is indeed an art—measuring the immeasurable. The tangible versus the intangible. Approaching time timelessly.

Is there a conduct of the highest order without control?

Beyond words?

The Relationship Challenge: This thought-provoking, emotion-unlocking, truth-unfolding state of inquiry. Seemingly simple. But designed to test Logic, Understanding, and Self-awareness, which are all the hallmarks of Order.

The Affection of Meditation.

I never felt a responsibility to say what Order is in Relationship, but instead, I felt compelled to question Disorder.

To answer that was to answer the question of Truth. Goodness. Wholesomeness.

Decency. Simplicity. Dignity.

Good manners.

What is Meditation in Relationship?

Presence. Integrity. Showing our True Nature.

It is the self-consciousness that looked toward the sun, and saw not just a life force, but time.

The immeasurable creating the measurable.

From sundial to clock—and with it, discipline.

Beware: Disorderliness stems from time. From our attempts to manipulate it. To immortalize it.

To compromise it.

Nature's Embrace. Connection. A Meditation.

What is Nature?

It sources light. It sources hope. Its spatiality gives birth to Rebirth—To Renewal—To Realization.

Divine Order. Grace. Humility.

Wisdom.

The Infinite. The Timeless. The Limitless.

A moment.

This one.

Moment by moment.

In and out of presence.

A complete but yet unfinished state of perceptivity.

Being conscious, moment by moment by moment.

Light, passing through a widening aperture, enlightens the soul, grazes the unconscious, sharpens clarity, seamlessly springing from within.

Upward. Onward to vulnerability.

The masks are off. I can see. I can hear.

I can feel your majesty.

Trillions and trillions and trillions of cells wander like vagabonds astray, bursting into life, awakened from dormancy. My attitude feels like it's being dusted off like dungarees hung alone in the barn.

You come alive, not to stay, not for long, for the moment.

Let's see what prayer was answered today.

Prayer without Meditation, like a half-truth, sits alone.

The artificial mind. The body brain. The cellular emotion. A Spiritual-Mind-Body connection rhythmically attuned. With one.

Depression has faded. It has completed its transition into wisdom.

Renewed. Anchored. At Peace.

You are so much more than when you say 'I am.'

The box—the boundaries—the limitation.

What if I told you that you've become an illusion of your imagination?

Delusional?

Doing the same thing over and over and over and over again, without expectation. Not insanity—a spiritual torpor.

Fast asleep.

How could one ignore the breath? Would you vandalize your own home?

What is the breadth of understanding without the breath of compassion?

Coasting along, looking for answers to questions that have barely been put together. The breath of life—the sun; the source of time, shining presence on one's precondition.

Look up to the heavens. Don't shoot for the moon. Don't aim for the stars.

Be Still.

Be Gentle.

Be Wise.

Patience awaits the Sun. The source of light. The source of time.

God's creation.

Meditation.

The Moon, the Stars, the Universe, the Sun within.

Conscious as the day, glorious as the night, from sunset to sunrise, the soul—the quiet self—is in beautification.

Listening with a second lease on life. Healing to the jubilation of Grace.

Seeing without distortion. Envisioning without haste.

Looking. Listening. Learning.

Alive.

Resist the urge to elongate. Temper the voice to manipulate.

Silence the thought to imitate, for you might miss the intention behind this moment, as attention evaporates.

Moment by moment by moment....

Words. Of. Wisdom.

Faith.

What is the Nature of Faith?

To "have faith" is not to grasp. It is not to claim, contain, or command.

To "have" means to honor. To receive. To abide.

Faith does not quantify. It does not qualify. It does not identify.

Faith is the art of letting go of the Known—the Past. It is the Innocence of the Unknown. An invitation to unlearn what you think you know.

Your Spiritual Practice isn't always what you do; it's also what you don't do.

Yes—creating space within the noise. Not cumulative. Not linear. One breath at a time.

Soul-searching. Soul-bearing. Soul-energizing. Soul-evolving.

The Virtues of the Inner Sense.

Discernment, not to escape trouble, but to avoid it altogether.

Discretion, not to silence judgment, but to exercise it.

Discipline, not of control, but of austerity.

This is not a means to an end. It is an ending with meaning.

A beginning.

Anew.

To think for yourself, you must see for yourself. To learn from impatience requires patience.

Faith is the willingness to confront what you don't know. To disembark from the status of knowledge and freshen what's possible.

A Wisdom Beyond Knowledge.

Yes. It is called Presence. It is this very moment.

Gentle. Meek. Mild.

Innocent.

Despite the intrusiveness of the Digital Revolution—which consumes so much of our time, space, and attention—restraint must be exercised, and patience must be preserved.

Be mindful. Be aware. Be graceful.

A constellation to uphold.

Hear the Soul's Whisper.

In the early dawn. Before daybreak, break the monotony of automation.

Be Still.

Listen.

Listen to the waves of your Soul. To the drumbeat of your Heart. To the chirping of the Mind—let it fly freely.

Faith is a Meditation.

Let it discern. Let it concern. Let it teach you discretion.

Faith is Beauty. It flowers in the Unknown.

An Inner Knowing.

Listen.

What would this world be without Meditation?

I will not disgrace it with my limitation. I will say this, though: Out of Meditation comes an innate Pursuit of Order.

Self-Awareness.

When asked, what is the difference between Prayer and Meditation? A Soul-wise Hummingbird Whisperer responded: "Prayer is you talking to God. Meditation is God speaking to you."

Patience isn't just a call to action. It's a call to attention.

To Listen. To Evolve. To have Faith.

And, nurture the Soul.

Meditate.

The Promise was not made to be kept. Like a lived truth, it was made to be explored. The future is not coded—it is relational. Of the heart and mind, not computational.

Of the Soul.

In the Now.

To be Present is to be Selfless.

Afterword

Toward Nurture: The Nature of Relationship

If *Atrophy of the Soul* was a descent into the pits of apathy, suffering in silence—where promises break apart, and patience is stretched thin—then what follows must be an ascent. Not a return to the chaos of the past, but a move toward passion. Compassion.

In the chapter "Nurture" from *A Dozen Roses*, we glimpsed the valuable lessons of tending: the slow, intentional act of remaining present when leaving might seem easier. The rose, once drooping, was not thrown away — it was watered. The soil, once dry, was not blamed — it was tilled. That spirit now becomes the seed of the next book: *NURTURE – The Nature of Relationship*.

Continuing the tradition of truth-seers, this new work may not provide answers but will reaffirm the authenticity of our questions. It aims to see relationships not as separate struggles but as one ongoing truth. It honors the seasons of intimacy—the bloom, the wilt, the compost, the rebirth—and recognizes that nurturing is the core of caring. It's not a performance but a spiritual practice of observation.

We will explore the archetypes that shape our relational lives: the mirror that reveals, the bridge that connects, the wound that teaches, and the garden that grows. We will ask what it means to love unconditionally, to listen without pretense, and to serve with purpose and intention.

If you've experienced atrophy, then you know that the nurturer is the one who is nurtured. Shall we tend the soil together—not to force possibilities, but to honor its divine timing?

—Charles H. Jarvis

www.ingramcontent.com/pod-product-compliance
Lightning Source LLC
Chambersburg PA
CBHW070148080526
44586CB00015B/1902